The Dance

Select Verses of
Elsie Lewis Eastman

Edited by
Rosemary Hyslop

Original poems by Elsie Lewis Eastman
Edited by Rosemary Hyslop

hysloprosemary@gmail.com
JesusAtoningLife.com

Cover photo by Billy Huynh on Unsplash
Cover and interior layout by Rachel Hall, WritelyDivided Editing & More

The Dance: Select Verses of Elsie Lewis Eastman / Rosemary Hyslop, Editor. —1st edition.

ISBN: 979-8-9863533-4-0 Paperback

In memory of my sister

Elsie (Hyslop) Lewis Eastman

October 4, 1936–February 26, 2008

Contents

Foreword

I decided to publish these verses of my sister, Elsie Lewis Eastman, because they capture something of the mystery and promise for God's creation which may prove to be a blessing to all who read them. Most of the verses were written a few years before she crossed over into Eternity. Just as a child who is fresh from God can reveal something of His Face, so may one who is close to ascending into His Presence. Did not our Savior tell us that unless we humble ourselves, becoming like a little child, we cannot enter the Kingdom of Heaven? (see Matthew 18:3–4).

As I read the thoughts she expressed in verse during those months approaching her demise, I remembered her sharing with me, so long ago, that she felt like what the psalmist expressed:

LORD, my heart is not haughty,
Nor my eyes lofty.
Neither do I concern myself with great matters,
Nor with things too profound for me.
Surely I have calmed and quieted my soul,
Like a weaned child with his mother;
Like a weaned child is my soul within me.

Psalm 131:1–2 NKJV

I am so glad that she also embraced the other creatures of our world as she explored the wonder of this life and the mystery of the great plan and purpose of our God and Father, fulfilled through His infinite Love for His whole Creation.

—Rosemary Hyslop
August 2023

The Dance

Then Jacob awoke from his sleep and said, "Surely the LORD is in this place, and I did not know it." He was afraid and said, "How awesome is this place! This is none other than the house of God, and this is the gate of heaven!"

Genesis 28:16–17 NASB1995

As Jacob went on his way, God's angels met him. When he saw them, Jacob said, "This is God's camp!" He named that place Mahanaim [Two Camps].

Genesis 32:1–2 GW

"Who is this that looks forth like the dawn,
fair as the moon, bright as the sun terrible as an army with banners?"

I went down to the nut orchard,
to look at the blossoms of the valley,
to see whether the vines had budded,
whether the pomegranates were in bloom.
Before I was aware, my fancy set me in a chariot beside my prince.

Return, return, O Shulammite,
return, return, that we may look upon you.

Why should you look upon the Shulammite,
as upon a dance before two armies?

Canticles 6:10–13 NRSV

Turning

Jesus said to her, 'Mary!' She turned and said to Him, 'Rabboni!' (which is to say, Teacher)

John 20:16, *paraphrased*

When I look back on my life and lives of others that I have known well, I observe that in spite of man's transgressions and deviations from the "Way" on my part or in the lives of others, the Way of the Lord in our hearts has been steadily ongoing through good and evil, or joy and suffering, or forgetfulness and neglect.

His creative work deep underneath all the surface chaos and wrong turnings has been progressing toward His loving purposes for us, without any "shadow of turning."

I wonder if that might not be true also of those who do not acknowledge him or believe in him. That in spite of themselves, the time might come when suddenly they might turn and see behind them the steady progress of an unseen, unrecognized work that will reveal a pattern, learned during the living, that could break out into the light of meaning, and reveal his constant hope and beautiful possibilities. Such is the "Way" of His steadfast mercy, forgiveness, purpose and love for us all.

—Elsie Lewis Eastman

2006

Preludes

And Moses said, I will turn aside now and see
this great sight, why the bush is not burnt.
And when Jehovah saw that he turned aside
to see, God called unto him out of the midst of the bush,
and said, Moses, Moses. And he said, Here am I.

Exodus 3:3–4 ASV

He called a child, set him in front
of them, and said, I tell you this:
unless you turn round and become like
children, you will never enter the kingdom of Heaven.

Matthew 18:2–3 NEB

With these words she turned round and saw
Jesus standing there, but did not recognize him.
Jesus said, 'Mary!' She turned to him and said,
'Rabbuni!' (which is Hebrew for 'My Master').

John 20:14, 16 NEB

One of them finding himself cured,
turned back praising God aloud.
He threw himself down at Jesus' feet and
thanked him. And he was a Samaritan.

Luke 17:16 NEB

The God Who Listens and Hopes

Thoughts on James Ch. 1, vv. 17-18

At our slightest turning, at the smallest yearning,
Any questioning, any wondering, any hoping —
Any beginning of love, our God is there waiting,
Receiving and responding to our offering,
To shower us with answers, satisfactions, understanding,
And greater hope, always more of his own
Fruitfulness, flowing life and love, given
Without any change of purpose
Or shadow of turning.

12/17/2006

Earth

Earth is a place
And also what
We are made of

I
SOJOURN

By faith he stayed for a time in the land he had been promised, as in a foreign land, living in tents, as did Isaac and Jacob, who were heirs with him of the same promise.

Hebrews 11:9 NRSV

Each of us wakes in a garden
Somewhere east in Eden
In the time between the two trees
Two trees in the garden
(Planted by the hand of God)
Two trees having different fruit
And growing in the same soil

Somewhere a poet has said
"It's strange to remember
That while we are here
We are always living and dying

At the same time"
In the middle way
In the time between the two trees
The garden has become a dark wood

Here is a dying—a dying to be born again
Not reincarnation
But responding to an invitation
To exchange mortality for eternity
Love born into the flesh invites us
To be born from the spirit – 'from above'

Not to renounce the gift of flesh
But desire its salvation
Not to put a stop to time
But an end to transience

II
HOME

Scarcely had I left them behind when I met my true love. I seized him and would not let him go until I had brought him to my mother's house, to the room of her who had conceived me.

Canticles 3:4 NEB

We would be like the Lord
To be like the Lord is to be like this:
He stayed with the world
To death on the cross.
He could have left us,
But he did not.
He stayed with us.
In like manner then
We would oh Lord
With you - - - stay here
For the joy that was set before you.
In this is the saving:
The staying.
Let us leave no one
Or no one thing behind
We pray.

You, oh Lord, are not willing
That any should perish.
With you, oh lord, let us stay
With you, we are safe.
Even when you are

Bound, blindfolded, flogged, slapped
Spit upon, mocked, scorned, hated,
And nailed to a wooden cross - - - pierced
Forsaken

Even there, only with you
Are we safe.
Let us stay with you oh Lord
Let us stay with you

2/27/2007

Listening for the God Who Speaks

Step by step we are led into understanding
Out of the comfort zone
What we have known
Where we have been
We hear the future
The unknown
The 'every word' of God calling us
Into the new

Our own yearning uproots us
The stirring the straining
The struggling
Desire
For more than knowledge
Love calls us
Sometimes into darkness
Only later into the light
Our love answers - - -
To know as we are known

Lord you saw the darkness
The darkness which you had made
You trusted yourself to the nature
That you had created
The process that your desire
had called into being
The darkness
The unknowing

Of the womb of the cosmos
The body of the virgin
She knew
she understood
You gave yourself
to unknowing
To closed eyes - - -
To your mother's knowing
to her faith her trusting
Her love

He knew you first
O God our father
like us
Through his mother's face
In your image
A face of love
Like all of us
From the seeing learning the unseen
Out of which
O Uncreated Light
We have our being

10/23/2007

The Creation of the Self

Life grows by expressing itself.

Jurgen Moltmann

I

We had to help in our coming to be –
He could have made puppets
He could have made slaves
But He had to help humans –
Become
What *He* wished to be
And *He*
Must always be free –
So must we be –
Thus we must help
In our coming to be

*****

I've dreamed a dream
Only God knows
If it's so - - -
Before He created
The world that we know
From the very beginning
He was wanting a body
For Himself – to become
He had wanted a mother

Both sisters and brothers
Many sons – many daughters –
He wanted a dwelling
A place which was Home
Among His own kind –
Flesh of His flesh
And bone of His bone

*****

From the beginning
He had loved His creation
And He chose to become –
A part of what
It
Had chosen to be

*****

This was a work
To be done – not by magic –
Raw power or strength
But by loving and nurture
And letting us be
As He said long ago
'Let there be' – 'Let there be'

*****

This is well-known
By any good parent
Watching and waiting
And holding the breath
At the first fearful footstep
Without holding on
Then beyond and beyond
They go

Full of hope
Taking new risks everyday –
Only love gives the strength
And the courage to know
Only taking the risk
Will allow them to grow

*****

So it is with our making
In cosmological scale –
From the very beginning
To where we are now
From the very beginning
He gave His own Life
To that which was coming
To be –
A life that was truly our own –
For creation was filled
From within – with a will
An emerging
Of freedom – of power
To grow
A gift truly given
From *His* Heart
To the Heart
Of the matter He made
A freedom of *blending* or *sharing*
Both God and creation
Both needing – responding
In the love and desire
We each had
For other

*****

From the beginning
He had loved His creation
And He chose to become –
A part of what
It
Had chosen to be

*****

(Sometimes I think
– Dust that I am –
That the reach of our being
Might go beyond space
Beyond cosmos or Heavens
Wherever He leads us
We can follow Him there)

*****

He waits and He watches
In patience and Love
His risk has been greater
Than even *He* knew
The gifts that He's given
To help us to grow
Have taken His All –
Again and again
The cause of all things
That are done by our God
Is His *Love* creating –
Love without end

*****

II

In Jesus –
God's heart is expressed
As He hung there to die
exhausted and emptied
As <u>we</u> had insisted
Holiness tested – perfected – on view
Jesus *stayed* – on the cross
Being faithful as God –
And faithful as Man –
– To both –
The Cosmos and God –
Salvation created
Mortality ended

*****

In Jesus –
Man's freedom chose God
God's freedom chose Man
Both fully expressed
Love fully exchanged
Each part of creation
In the newness he wrought
Is called into fullness –
And so we must use
The life that He made
When He made his life here
His prayers and ours
Are now being answered –
His kingdom *will* come
His will *will be* done

On earth
As in Heaven
He waits and He watches
And we're waiting too –
Being still as we listen –
While we work out our own
Salvation – with Him –
– In our hearts –
The cosmos is waiting
For our resurrection –
And we wait –
for it too

11/17/07

Changing

Love is very everything, like fire:
Many things burning,
But only one combustion.

from "Echoes" by Laura Riding[1]

At times in our dreams we will walk
Down the corralled corridors of our minds
With either men or angels,
The living or the dead;
We often know not whom nor which.

I've once seen birds when walking there.
Their heads were wrapped in whirling flame;
While I was weeping for the birds
One sweetly spoke to me and said
That she was neither burned nor dead.

I wonder then, if here
We may speak with angels unaware;
Or if the dead may visit with us,
And we can neither see
Nor know them to be there.

So Too, do hot and holy fires rage around us,
Flames of purest life and gold;

[1] The poem can be found translated by Rodrigo Garcia Lopez in Laura Riding's *Mindscapes: Poemas,* São Paulo, Brasil: Iluminuras, 2004, p. 90.

Or in our midst, but seldom seen and rarely noticed,
Is tender burning love transforming without ceasing?
Toward which, we may be cold - - - and still not know it.

Have we somehow failed to sense so near us
Ministers of fire flaming, or failed to feel within our hearts
The deep foundations of the mountains fiercely burning?
Purifying transformations, new beginnings
Bringing into being - - - the New Creation.

12/18/2007

Cosmos

The heavens are telling the glory of God
And the firmament shows the work of his hands
Day to day pours out speech
and night to night reveals knowledge.
They are no earthly speech or words;
Their voice cannot be heard.
Yet their music goes out through
all the earth and their words to the
end of the world.

Psalm 19:1–4, *paraphrased*

Lord, your name is spread over all the earth.
You speak to us through the stars.
The Child born under the Star,
Given to us, o Lord,
Was made of the dust
Of this dear earth.
The earth is made
Of the dust of the stars.
The wounded body
Which even now is yours,
Was woven
In the depths of the earth.
The Word became
Stardust,
This is still
Your resurrected
Flesh.

12/22/2007

On the Life and Death of Jesus of Nazareth

Jesus showed us that God could be truly God in His fullness,
without omniscience, omnipotence or omnipresence;
that the most important things about God are other things –
that He can cause and allow Himself to be vulnerable,
to love, suffering, time, change and death, and still be God;
exhibiting in these deprivations, the fullest revelation of
His creative righteousness, power, and love.

Date unknown

Thoughts Upon Reading Psalm 109

O Lord Christ
Did you learn from the Psalms
What Gethsemane would mean?
When you read in synagogue
The words of condemnation of evil
The hatred of evil
by the good man
And by your Father in heaven
Did you take them upon yourself?
Did you feel your kinship with us
(In our evil)
As a wound to your love for us
To your heart
Your love
never ending and constant
Feeling our sin
In your tender flesh?
The great drops of blood
On Gethsemane's earth
Sinking into the earth
of which you too are made
You who made the worlds
O Lord
you redeem not only our evil
but also our good
You bore it all in your holy flesh
You who were made sin for us
And have made *all things* new

O Lord God, help us to see all of reality with your love, with the mind which was and is in you, Lord Jesus. Redeem all things, O Lord, we pray. We live in your hope. It is ours.

10/3/2007

A poem in Haiku form

The Cross on Golgotha

Always – Love is new
It is action – it is change
It goes out – it stays

Jerusalem is
The place – where God became man
And man became – God

He'd said – before death
'I have finished the work that
You gave me to do'

He died – a man's death
Why have you – forsaken me?
He asked a man's God

The Father was still
He knew – that Jesus – alone
Had finished God's work

He'd said – before death
'I am – the Resurrection'
He rose the God – Man

He said – 'Follow me'
We enter His Work – The Life
He'd made – given – to us

11/6/2007

The Cry of Dereliction

God became a child
The child grew into a man.

The Spirit of God
Always with him – as with man;
At his baptism
Descended with power
upon him
Anointing him; –

At the cross
Became silent
To him.

The Son of Man
Stayed – alone;
As God – as Man
The Savior of the world.
A Man became God.

O the loneliness
Of God.

11/11/2007

New and Revised Haiku

11/06/1978

Like the kindly kiss
Of an austere grandmother
Sun so pale today

Summer, 1996

This morning each thought
Has the crystal resonance
Of a bell – nearby

10/25/2007

Late October days
Redolent of dying leaves - -
Of other autumns

10/25/2007

The word comes to us
We nurture – it grows
From our life   A poem – born

——≈——

10/30/2007

The maker should know
When touching the living gift
That he might kill it

——≈——

11/10/2007

I was a painter
Of pears pots – golden quinces
Looking for stillness

Now I'm a seeker
Of Fire and Wind – bringing word
Of Eternity

——≈——

11/10/2007

The sweetness – and pain
Of transience – to hold in
The heart forever

Time in memory
Anchored in pillars of gold
God's future is ours

———≈———

11/11/2007

Movement of music
The stillness of paintings
The Eternal – here

The meaning of word
Unites now and the future
Carrying the past

Feast of Bread and Wine
Presence of God – with us
God desires to stay

For both God and man
Memory of suffering –
Treasure forever

We would follow Him
The God who learned to obey
Through His suffering

The path to freedom
is not power or knowledge
But Love in the heart

Love is the Healer
Love is the Guide and Teacher –
The deep Heart of God

11/11/2007

The Japanese find
Beauty in transience – and
God works redemption

11/13/2007

Shining golden day!
Emboldened leaves face the sun
Light blends earth and sky

Linger – air of gold
Too soon the fallen leaves – will
Color our footprints

Brazen with beauty
Leaves vie with the dying sun
In cool autumn light

11/21/2007

Cloud and mist surround
The last leaves of late autumn
Days of grey and gold

Late Summer 1996 - 12/06/2007

Like cloud wisps – words drift
On wings of light – revealing –
Just whispers – but light

11/30/2007

Three things are teachers
Gifts from earth and the Lord God
Love – suffering – joy

Thoughts on a Fiftieth Year Class Reunion

Perhaps
In these days of aging and waiting
In some trepidation and some expectation
This has been
a taste of paradise

Each one of us
Singular — only himself
Like no other
seen from a long view
(Over half a century)
Precious to all the rest of us

The long slow days of childhood and youth
the miseries the ecstasies the boredom
the first tastes of life in the big world
the world of our peers
Blurred
And woven into a whole cloth
worn by each of us - -
A shared memory

Slights and hurts are all forgiven
Rivalries and envies and proud hearts
Conquered
by the hard and lovely lessons
of life and time
Nothing really lost
Through the many years

But all wrapped
By the bonds of love
into a gift
A blessing
To carry with us
Into eternity

7/31/2004

The Arts - - - In an Antique Shop

A lovely old thing
A funny little picture
In a tired old frame
Chipped and really quite shabby
A sort of Victorian valentine
A romantic collage
A kind of message? Maybe
Touching a memory
From something forgotten
Perhaps like a poem
Or a soft low voice
Reading a poem
A gentle murmuring sound
In another language
That you don't understand
Or you can't quite hear the words
For they're lost in the air
Drifting somewhere in time
Like a melody lingering
With the scent of dried roses
Rather haunting, you know?
Or maybe you do hear the meaning
There just are no words
I guess it really doesn't need - - -
to say any more

10/30/2007

November

Delicate November
　　With your pale thin face
Your voice is hushed and whispering
　　Like a house
　　　　When the people are fled

The air rustles your hair
　　With a silvery sound
Fragile and receding
　　Like a bell
　　　　On a faraway hill

Your somber tattered gown
　　　　Flutters in the wind
Wan umbers and ochres
　　And watery green
　　　　Mingling with shadows

Delicate November
　　As you turn from me
Your look is remote yet lingering
　　Like memories of pleasures
　　　　Of other years

11/1/1979

Factory Farming

Has anyone given thanks?
So many millions of suffering food animals
In the 'civilized' world
All things of meaning in life *for* them
We have taken *from* them
Except the eating and the suffering
Toward the end
Even the eating is a suffering
Nothing left
But the *sacrifice*

One thing only
We cannot take from them - - -
Their innocence

11/8/2007

Then I Knew

Into the parking lot
Out of the grocery store
To get to my car
An animal sound
Like a barking dog
At first I thought it close by
But looking up
Toward the hillside
I saw that way off
At the very top
Of a spindly fragile pine
Stretching scrawny bare branches
Into the sky
There was a bird

Then I knew that it was a crow
Perched there
Calling out
Then I knew - - -

It is so good
Thought the black black crow
When you feel like sounding off
To fly to the very top
Of all that you see
To the top
Of the very tallest tree
And cry
Caw Caw Caw

Brother Crow
9/27/07

A Cat Story About Doors

Cats can be strange;
(Somewhat like us).
But it can scarce be believed
How they so want to be
On the other side
Of any closed door
Except for
The door - - the other side of - -
Achieved!

When they've got the victory
They must explore
Then explore more
Of the great mystery
Of the far side
Of the door;
But don't even try
To catch them - -
Just leave them
Then close the door.

And in this room most forbidden
(In delightful discovery),
They feel nicely hidden
and almost forgotten
Somewhere down dark and under,
While they lurk there all wrapped-in
Ecstasy and wonder, - -

Much musing meditation - -
(So - *Feline*).
And there they remain
ignoring your calling - -
Till dinner time.

1/7/08

To Arabel

My little trudger cat!
Your head bobs as you walk
As one who labors
But your footstep is so slight
Stepping softly softly
My sweet silken trudger cat

2/7/07

Prayer of Hope

Lord teach us to be among your innocent ones
Blessed and dressed in white robes
of your own making
Give me a heart trustworthy like your own
So that the good and holy
May live in peace and safety with me
Hold me my Lord
In your perfect and vulnerable love
That you may be
Forever safe *from* me
As I dwell in the freedom
which is your hope for me - - -
And for all your creation which you love
Lord keep us always
That we may be a home
For your dwelling and rest
For you who have called one of us – Mother

10/16/07

Elsie Lewis Eastman ~ Biography

Whether sculpting an object from a bar of Ivory Soap, drawing a person's face on a piece of scrap paper, or capturing the imagination of her cousins and younger sister with her made-up-as-you-go storytelling, Elsie excelled at anything she proposed to do. She grew up in St. Clairsville, a town in east central Ohio, graduating Valedictorian of her class. Wife, mother, artist, and poet, Elsie was a hidden gem. But greater than any intellectual or artistic achievement is the human soul which can be seen and felt in her verses. Elsie Lewis Eastman, who did not seek great things for herself (see Foreword), had a soul that, in measure known only to God, magnified Him (see Luke 1:46).

About the Editor

Rosemary Hyslop decided to follow the Lord Jesus Christ as a teenager. She had access to the excellent library of her father, James Hyslop, who was a learned teacher of the Word. Inspired by her father's understanding and teaching of the Person of Christ, she continued to study the Bible in depth, as well as study to be a nurse. She received her Bachelor's in nursing, hoping to use her medical knowledge as a Christian missionary. She worked in a mission hospital in the Holy Land for only one year, returning home due to an illness in her family that required her care.

Believing that her mission was not abroad but at home, Rosemary used her nursing skills to care for her family while continuing her biblical studies. Many years later, she moved from her home in east central Ohio to a Christian community in north central Florida, where she has lived for almost two decades.

Rosemary has been writing on biblical subjects for the last ten years, posting her studies on her web page jesusatoninglife.com. She has published two books, *God's Humanity: The Shocking Wonder of the Incarnation* (2022) and *The Atonement: Punishment or Person?* (2023).

Rosemary shares what she sees in the Word, hoping others may deepen their understanding of the Christian life. Passionate about the "greatness of salvation" (Hebrews 2:3) found only in the Lord Jesus Christ, she earnestly believes that the Church must not only grow outward but upward (Hebrews 6:1).

For more inspirational reading,
please visit Rosemary Hyslop's website:

JesusAtoningLife.com

www.ingramcontent.com/pod-product-compliance
Lightning Source LLC
LaVergne TN
LVHW090134160826
845673LV00017B/2468